TONFA
Karate Weapon of Self-Defense

by Fumio Demura

Edited by Gregory Lee
Graphic Design by Karen Massad

©Ohara Publications, Incorporated 1982
All rights reserved
Printed in the United States of America
Library of Congress, Catalog Card No. 82-81557
ISBN No. 0-89750-080-6

Fifteenth printing 1993

WARNING

OHARA ▯ PUBLICATIONS, INCORPORATED

SANTA CLARITA, CALIFORNIA

ACKNOWLEDGEMENTS

I would like to express my thanks to Gladys Caldwell and Dwight Lomayasva for their help in the preparation of this book; and to my excellent students, Chuck Lanza and Kiyoshi Kusuhara for their assistance as my partners in the photographs. My appreciation also to the staff of Ohara Publications.

DEDICATION

To the late Okinawan karate and kobudo master, Kenshin Taira, that perfect example of the gentle spirit of the martial arts, who was initially responsible for my interest and subsequent skill in kobudo; to Ryusho Sakagami and Kenwa Mabuni, revered masters who are the founders of modern kobudo and karate; and to Masu Demura, my honored mother, for her constant mental inspiration.

ABOUT THE AUTHOR

Fumio Demura, fifth-dan, is one of the most highly respected karateka in the world today. His strenuous schedule of demonstrations has made him an ambassador in the world of karate, taking him from Europe and the Middle East to Central America and Australia.

Born in Yokohama, Japan, Demura first studied kendo in grammar school, progressing during his school years from karate and aikido to judo. While at Nihon University in Tokyo, he earned a Bachelor of Science degree in economics. At the same time, he developed his special interest in kobudo, including the use of such weapons as the bo, the sai, the nunchaku, the tonfa and the kama. Demura studied kobudo under the tutelage of Kenshin Taira and Ryusho Sakagami.

His reputation as a champion was secured in 1961 when he won the All-Japan Karate Freestyle Tournament, and for three consecutive years thereafter he was rated as one of Japan's top eight competitors. His many tournament wins include the East Japan, the Shito-Ryu Annual and the Kanto District championships. Demura has also received the All-Japan Karate Federation President's trophy for outstanding tournament play, and he has been awarded certificates of recognition from Japanese Cabinet officials for his contributions to the art of karate.

In 1965, Demura came to the United States at the invitation of Dan Ivan to teach Shito-Ryu, one of the world's four major systems of karate.

Demura has entertained and educated thousands of people since 1968 at such diverse places as the Japanese Village and Deer Park in Buena Park, California; Marineland; Disneyland; the Las Vegas Hilton; and even the Playboy Club in New York City. He has appeared as a stunt man in films, including *The Island of Dr. Moreau.*

BLACK BELT Magazine's Hall of Fame has twice honored Fumio Demura, once in 1969 when he was named Karate Sensei of the Year and in 1975 when he was honored as Martial Artist of the Year. He has also won the martial arts' Golden Fist Award (1973).

Since 1970, Demura has authored five books, beginning with *Shito-Ryu Karate.* His books on kobudo include *Nunchaku* (1971), *Sai* (1974), *Bo* (1976) and *Advanced Nunchaku* with Dan Ivan (1977).

HISTORY

During the 17th century, the people of Okinawa were pro-
hibited from using weapons such as knives, swords and
spears by the invading government of Japan. The lack of
workable metal in the Ryukyu Islands added to the scarcity of weapons in Okinawa. This condition, and the need for personal protection,
stimulated the development of the Okinawan martial arts: *karate* and
kobudo.

Most kobudo weapons were originally farm implements, in-
geniously converted into effective weapons of self-defense. The *nunchaku,* the *bo* and the *tonfa* are three examples. The nunchaku, con-
structed of two hardwood sticks secured together at one end by a
braided rope, could be used either to pound grain or to strike, block
and pinch. The bo may originally have been the *tenbin,* a staff used to
carry buckets of water on the shoulders. It's use as a powerful striking
and blocking weapon with greater reach is obvious.

The tonfa, or *toifa* (handle), was originally a wooden handle fitted
into a hole on the side of a millstone used by the Okinawans for mill-
ing grain. This handle, which was easily disengaged from the millstone, became a very effective weapon of defense. The main part of
the tonfa, or millstone handle, consists of a largle hardwood body
about 15 to 20 inches in length and a smaller cylindrical grip secured
at a right angle to the main body about six inches from one end.

The early practitioners of the Okinawan martial arts foresaw these
weapons as an extension of their hand techniques, and quickly
adopted these weapons into their training.

Karate and kobudo are mutually supportive practices; the knowledge of both skills can improve the student's techniques immensely.
Without a thorough knowledge of karate basics, the tonfa student is
severely limited in his development. By the same token, improve-
ment in the use of the tonfa extends the attacks and strengthens the
blocks of the karate student. Continued practice with the tonfa can
help improve balance, coordination and physical strength.

CONTENTS

Chapter I: INTRODUCTION TO THE TONFA 11

Chapter II: TONFA STANCES 17

Chapter III: KARATE AND TONFA SIMILARITIES 27

Chapter IV: TONFA STRIKING TECHNIQUES 49

Chapter V: SELF-DEFENSE APPLICATIONS 81

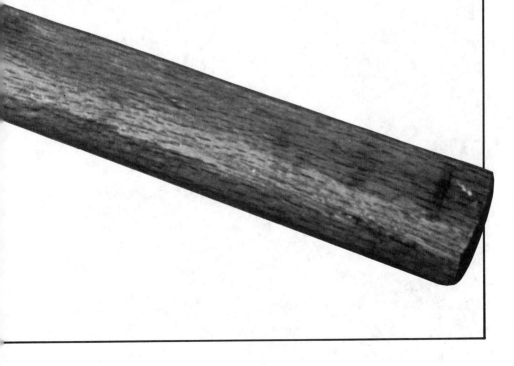

INTRODUCTION TO THE TONFA

Though not as flashy or as glamorous as the nunchaku, the tonfa is nevertheless an important tool in the kobudo tradition. Two tonfa in the hands of an expert make a poetic and graceful contribution to the art of *kata*.

The tonfa is also an excellent tool for the development of stronger hands and wrists, essential for achieving necessary power in blocking and striking in empty-hand techniques. This is where the tonfa is particularly desirable in practice over such weapons as the bo or nunchaku.

Swinging the tonfa requires a snap of the wrist not unlike that used in the last instant of a karate punch. By developing control—for instance, learning to stop the swivel motion of the tonfa by gripping the handle harder—hand strength will improve rapidly.

In this section, a basic introduction to the tonfa is provided. It is recommended that a karate student not begin practice with this or other kobudo implements until he or she has had at least several years of karate training.

ANATOMY OF THE TONFA

In order to deliver or receive a powerful blow, the parts of the tonfa must be strong, yet flexible. Several hardwoods which are not too brittle will satisfy this requirement, with the most popular materials being oak and cherry wood.

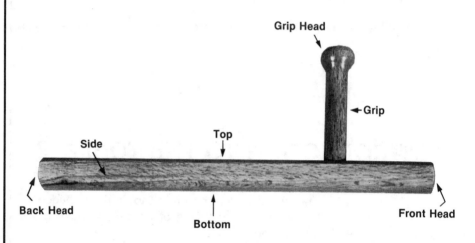

The length of the tonfa is determined from the grip to the back head. While holding the tonfa, the back head should extend past the elbow by about one-half inch. Once this distance is determined, the balance of the tonfa can be adjusted by reducing the length from the grip to the front head. Under these requirements, one must choose a length and balance to fit his physical characteristics and strength.

CARE OF THE TONFA

Normally, the tonfa is made of oak and consequently is very sturdy, but the connection between the grip and the main body can be a source of weakness. This location should always be checked before each practice to prevent injuries. The tonfa can also be varnished, if desired, and should be cleaned periodically with a cloth moistened with olive or other vegetable oil.

TYPES OF TONFA

Though the basic configuration of all tonfa is the same, with the small grip attached near one end of the weapon, the main body of the tonfa can be found in varied shapes. The illustrations below show some of the more common ones.

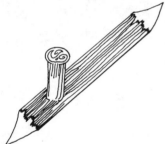

The square tonfa has four distinct faces on the main body, forming a long rectangle.

The top edge of the main body in this tonfa is flat, while the sides and bottom are rounded, forming a semicircle. This is the most popular tonfa shape.

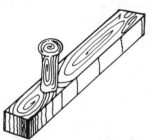

A crude, pointed tonfa with both back and front heads ending in a point which can be used for stabbing defenses.

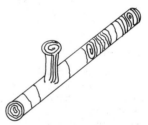

The main body of this tonfa is completely round from end-to-end.

A paddle-shaped tonfa, with the back head considerably wider than the front head.

The portion of the main body attached below the grip is wider and flatter than the rest of the body, which is round.

GRIPPING THE TONFA

The grasp of the tonfa resembles the karate fist. The grip is held loosely, yet firm enough so that the weapon is not dropped while in use. This somewhat loose hold allows the tonfa grip to move easily in the palm of the hand. At the moment of a strike or block one should squeeze or tighten the fingers around the tonfa grip to form a tight fist. To be effective with the weapon, the practitioner should develop

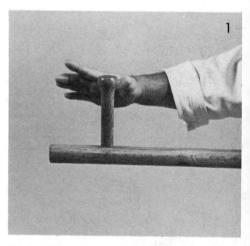

THE GRASP

Place the grip of the tonfa (1) between the thumb and the index finger. (2) Place the palm of the hand on the grip. (3) Close the fingers over the grip. (4) Be sure the thumb is on top of the index finger, as if making a fist. (5) Touch the top of the tonfa, back head end, to the elbow. (6) Front view of the tonfa adjusted correctly to the elbow.

strength in his wrist. This development will aid in the practitioner's karate training.

When swinging the tonfa it is critical to remember that minimal bending of the elbow is absolutely essential to avoid striking yourself with the weapon. Great care must be taken to keep the arms extended when rotating the tonfa.

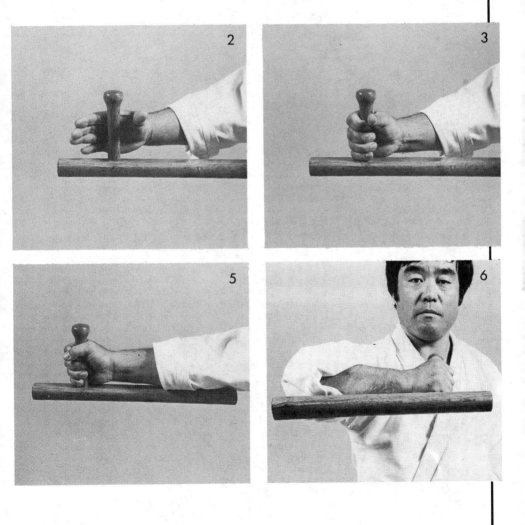

Chapter II

TONFA STANCES

The stances reviewed in this chapter are identical to those used in karate. Proper balance and maintaining good hip position is as essential in kobudo practice with the tonfa as in karate. Some of the stances, such as the *heiko-dachi, kiba-dachi* and *zenkutsu-dachi,* will be familiar to students of karate. Other stances, for example, the *T-dachi,* have been omitted because they have limited practical application in use with the tonfa.

Any stance should never be thought of as a decoration, but as a foundation for an effective, strong defense.

HEISOKU-DACHI
(Attention Stance)

A ready position in which your feet are together and arms at your sides. This stance places the student in a proper position from which to bow.

MUSUBI-DACHI
(Attention Stance— feet out)

A ready position in which your heels are together and toes pointed outward forming right angles. Your arms are slightly forward, gripping the tonfa.

HEIKO-DACHI
(Open Parallel Stance)

A natural position in which your feet are spread slightly apart approximately shoulder width, with the toes pointed forward.

SOTO-HACHIJI-DACHI
(Outward Open Leg Stance)

A natural position similar to the heiko-dachi, except that the toes are pointed outward.

UCHI-HACHIJI-DACHI
(Inverted Open Leg Stance)

The heels are separated about shoulder width and the feet are turned inward at a 45-degree angle.

SANCHIN-DACHI
(Hourglass Stance)

An inside, tensed stance in which your legs are spread slightly apart about shoulder width with the toes pointed inward. One foot should be placed slightly forward so that the heel of the forward foot is in line with the toes of the back foot.

REI-NO-JI-DACHI
(V-Stance)

The front foot is placed half a step ahead and in line with the back foot. The toes of the front foot are pointed straight ahead while the toes of the back foot are angled 45-degrees out.

KIBA-DACHI
(Horse Riding Stance)

The toes are turned inward, knees bent, and the hips thrust forward, pushing the lower stomach area to the front.

SHIKO-DACHI
(Square Stance)

This stance is almost the same as the kiba-dachi or horse riding stance except that the feet are turned outward at a 45-degree angle and the hips are dropped lower.

ZENKUTSU-DACHI
(Forward Stance)

This forward stance is widely used with attacks. Put most of your weight on your front leg while your back leg pushes forward. The shoulders remain squared.

GYAKU-ZENKUTSU-DACHI
(Rear Defense Stance)

This stance is used to retreat from attack from the rear. Weight distribution and foot positions are the same as in the zenkutsu-dachi or forward stance.

KOKUTSU-DACHI
(Back Stance)

This stance is used to defend against a frontal attack. Put most of your weight on your rear leg so that it may be used for support. The front foot points straight ahead, the back foot angled out at 90-degrees.

SAGI-ASHI-DACHI
(Crane Stance)

This stance is used mostly to defend against foot-sweeps or any attacks to the legs. Raise the leg being attacked and shift your body back out of range at the same time. The leg on which you are standing should be slightly bent, with your raised leg hooked behind the bend in the knee.

NEKO-ASHI-DACHI
(Cat Stance)

This stance emphasizes maneuverability, allowing you to kick with your forward leg in combination with your tonfa strike or block. Ninety percent of your weight is placed on the rear leg, leaving your forward leg flexible for attack.

FUDO-DACHI
(Immovable Stance)

This stance is similar to the zenkutsu-dachi, but the back leg is bent slightly and the hips twisted away from the front position. Both knees must be bent at approximately the same angle. This firm stance distributes the weight of the body equally between the legs.

KOUSA-DACHI
(Crossed-Leg Stance)

This stance is especially useful in a movement from a higher level position to a lower level attack or defense position. Your front foot should be planted flat on the floor while your back foot rests only on the toes.

Chapter III

KARATE AND TONFA SIMILARITIES

This chapter will contrast the basic blocks and strikes that are used in both karate and in tonfa practice. Since the tonfa is an extension of the hand, almost every karate technique can be duplicated with the tonfa. Your knowledge and skill in karate has a parallel in the use of the tonfa, and it will help improve your tonfa skills.

Note particularly the hand, fist and feet positions in these sections comparing blocking and striking movements both in empty hand and tonfa application.

UPWARD BLOCK

In karate, the forearm is used to block a face punch. With the tonfa, the grip is held firmly, protecting the underside of the forearm,

INSIDE FOREARM BLOCK

In karate, an inside forearm block can block a punch. With the tonfa held tightly by the grip, the defender uses the bottom edge of the

OUTSIDE FOREARM BLOCK

In karate, an outside forearm block can also block a punch. With the tonfa held firmly by the grip, the defender uses the bottom

and the defender can deflect a *bo* (staff) strike using an upward forearm block. The bottom edge of the tonfa deflects the blow.

AGE-UKE

weapon along his forearm to deflect a thrusting attack with the bo. The tonfa is held vertically, back head pointed down.

UCHI-YOKO-UKE

edge of the weapon along his forearm to deflect a bo thrust to the chest. The tonfa is held vertically, back head pointed down.

SOTO-YOKO-UKE

DOWNWARD BLOCK

In karate, the downward block is effective against punches or kicks to the midsection. With the tonfa, a bo thrust can be blocked

KNIFE-HAND BLOCK

In karate, the outside edge of the palm is used to block an attack. With the tonfa, a thrust to the chest area can

UPWARD CROSS BLOCK —HANDS OPEN

In karate, the palms are held open and the fingers point up in executing an open-hand cross block upward. Against a bo strike to

using the bottom edge of the tonfa, with the grip held firmly and the front head of the tonfa pointing down.

HARAI-UKE

be blocked using the bottom edge of the weapon, back head pointing down.

SHUTO-UKE

the face, the defender uses the bottom edge of both tonfa to block, back heads pointed up and away from the defender.

KOUSA-UKE

UPWARD CROSS BLOCK —HANDS CLOSED

In karate, the hands can be closed when executing an upward cross block. With the tonfa, the defender blocks the bo strike to the head or face with the bot-

DOWNWARD CROSS BLOCK—HANDS OPEN

In karate, the palms are held open and the fingers point down when executing an open-hand cross block downward. Against a bo strike to the stomach or

DOWNWARD CROSS BLOCK—HANDS CLOSED

In karate, the hands can be closed when executing a downward cross block. With the tonfa, the defender blocks a bo strike to the stomach or groin with the

tom edge as the point of contact and the back heads pointing down. The weapon protects the outside of both forearms. Note the strong stance.

KOUSA-UKE

groin, the defender uses the bottom edge of both tonfa to block, back heads pointed down and away from the defender.

KOUSA-UKE

bottom edge as the point of contact and the front heads of both tonfa pointing down. The weapon protects the outside of both forearms.

KOUSA-UKE

SIDE CROSS BLOCK— HANDS CLOSED

In karate, a punch can be deflected to the side using a cross hand block. With the tonfa, the defender can deflect a bo thrust to the chest area with the front

OUTWARD BLOCK—UP

In karate, the knife hand can block a face punch. With the tonfa, the defender flips the back head of the tonfa out to block a bo

OUTWARD BLOCK— DOWN

In karate, a knife hand block down can block a kick to the midsection. With the tonfa, the defender flips the back head of the tonfa out

heads of the tonfa pointing away and the bottom edge of each tonfa making contact. The body of the weapon protects the forearms.

KOUSA-UKE

strike to the head, deflecting the attack to the outside. The side edge of the tonfa is the point of contact.

FURI-UKE

and down to block a bo strike to the legs, deflecting the attack. The side edge of the tonfa is the point of contact.

FURI-UKE

35

DOUBLE FOREARM BLOCK

In karate, both forearms can be used to block a punch. With the tonfa, the defender can use the bottom edges of each tonfa to

PRESSING BLOCK

In karate, a horizontal pressing block with the forearm can block a punch. With the tonfa held by the grip and protecting the outside of

PALM/HEEL BLOCK

In karate, the heels of both palms, cupped together, can block a kick. With the tonfa held in one hand by

deflect a bo strike to the chest area, back heads pointing down and the body of the weapon protecting the outside of his forearms.

MOROTE-UKE

the forearm, the weapon can block a perpendicular thrust with a bo. The bottom edge of the weapon is the point of contact.

OSAE-UKE

the grip and the other hand grasping the back head, a bo thrust upward into the groin area can be blocked.

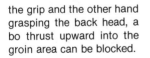

TEISHO-UKE

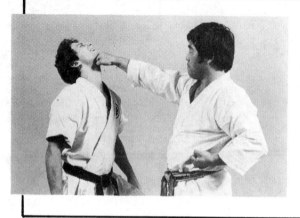

PUNCH

In karate, a direct punch to the chest or face area. With the tonfa, the front head is driven directly into the op-

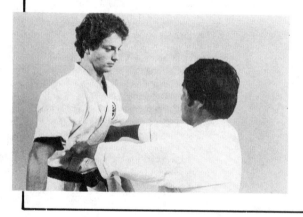

DOUBLE PUNCH

In karate, both fists can be thrust into the chest or stomach area. With the ton-fa, the front heads of both

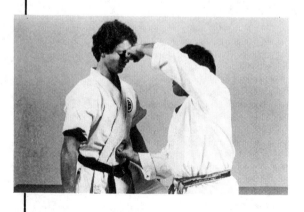

U-PUNCH

In karate, the fists can be thrust forward, one in an upward circular motion, the other down and under, into the face and stomach of the opponent, forming a U-shape with the arms. With

ponent's face in the same manner, with the body of the weapon underneath the forearm.

SEIKEN-ZUKI

tonfa can be thrust into the opponent's midsection. The body of the tonfa is underneath your forearms.

MOROTE-ZUKI

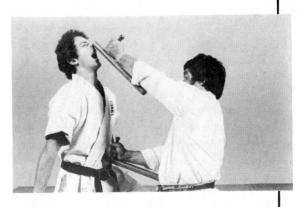

the tonfa, the front heads are driven into the target areas maintaining a firm hold on each grip, with the body of the tonfa underneath the forearms.

YAMA-ZUKI

SCISSORS PUNCH

In karate, the fists strike simultaneously on either side of the temples. With the tonfa, the front heads

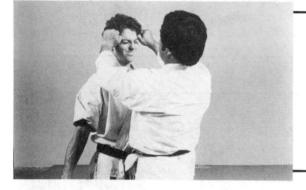

SCISSORS PUNCH II

In karate, the fists strike simultaneously on either side of the temples. With the tonfa, the grip heads

KNIFE-HAND STRIKE

In karate, the knife hand can strike the temple. Using the tonfa, the back head of the tonfa is flipped sideways in a circular manner,

HAMMER STRIKE

In karate, the hammer fist strikes an opponent behind the head. With the tonfa, the portion of the bottom edge beneath the grip head is used as the point of con-

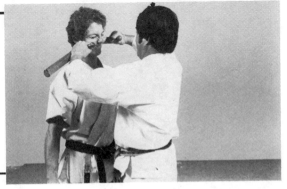

can be used to execute this blow, with the body of the weapon outside the fore-arms.

HASAMI-ZUKI

are used to execute the blow, with the body of the weapon on the outside of the forearms.

HASAMI-ZUKI

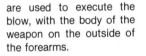

striking the opponent in the head. The side edge of the tonfa is the point of contact.

SHUTO-UCHI

tact, striking the opponent with a downward motion. The body of the tonfa is supported underneath the forearm.

TETTSUI

UPPERCUT STRIKE

In karate, the uppercut fist can deliver a blow on the chin. Using the tonfa, the front head of the tonfa is

BACK HAND

In karate, the back hand can be used to strike an opponent in the eyes with the knuckles as the point of contact. With the tonfa, the body of the tonfa is flipped

SPEAR HAND

In karate, the spear hand can be used to jab the eyes with the fingers extended. With the tonfa, the back

INSIDE RIDGE HAND

In karate, the area between the thumb and first finger is used to deliver a ridge hand strike to the throat. With the tonfa, the surfaces between the grip head and the front

driven into the chin held by the grip head, and the body of the weapon protects the outside of the forearm.

AGE-ZUKI

in a circular motion by holding the grip of the tonfa and swinging the back head of the weapon into the opponent's face. The side edge is the point of contact.

URAKEN

head of the tonfa can be thrust forward in a straight, punching fashion.

NUKITE

head of the tonfa can be used to strike the throat while gripping the body of the weapon from the back head end.

HIRABASAMI

43

UPWARD ELBOW STRIKE

In karate, an uppercut motion with the elbow strikes the opponent under the chin. Using the bottom edge of the tonfa near the

ELBOW STRIKE TO THE SIDE

In karate, a side elbow strike sweeps across the chest and strikes the opponent in the solar plexus. Using the tonfa in similar fash-

ELBOW STRIKE TO THE REAR

In karate, an elbow strike to the rear is delivered directly behind from the waist into the opponent's stomach area. When thrusting with the tonfa, the back head

DOWNWARD ELBOW STRIKE

In karate, the elbow can be driven downward in a strike to the back of an opponent's head. With the tonfa, the back head is thrust

back head, the weapon can be thrust into the opponent's chin with an upward, circular motion.

AGE-HIJIATE

ion, the back head of the tonfa can be thrust into the same area, maintaining a tight grasp on the grip head.

YOKO-HIJIATE

strikes the stomach area while the weapon is gripped close to the body with the tonfa underneath the forearm.

USHIRO-HIJIATE

downward, front head pointing up and the body of the weapon along the forearm.

OTOSHI-HIJIATE

ROUNDHOUSE ELBOW STRIKE

In karate, a backward circular motion drives the elbow into the jaw of an opponent. With the tonfa, the

EAGLE HAND STRIKE —UP

In karate, an eagle hand strike can be used to strike an opponent under the chin. With the tonfa, the palm grasps the body of the

EAGLE HAND STRIKE —DOWN

In karate, an eagle hand can be thrust downward into the eyes of the opponent. With the tonfa, the tonfa is

FOREARM STRIKE

In karate, a punch can be deflected using both forearms and simultaneously striking the back of the elbow and the inside of the wrist. With the tonfa, the

back head of the tonfa is thrust back in the same manner. The grip head must be held tightly.

MAWASHI-HIJIATE

tonfa near the back head and snaps the grip head of the weapon into the target area in a circular motion.

WASHITE (AGE)

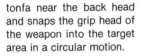

grasped near the back head and the grip head snapped downward into the eyes.

WASHITE (OTOSHI)

front heads are pointed up and the tonfa is held by the grips. The bottom edge of the tonfa is the point of contact.

KOTE-UCHI

Chapter IV

TONFA STRIKING TECHNIQUES

The use of the tonfa in striking is varied and can be adapted for one or two tonfa techniques. This chapter details the flipping and swinging motions of tonfa and their correct execution. Learning the use of the tonfa requires a great deal of practice, as the beginner must learn how to whip the tonfa without striking himself.

Pay close attention to the positions of the hands, elbows and feet in each sequence of photographs.

SEIKEN-ZUKI
(Punch)

The front head of the tonfa is driven directly into the target (1-3) in the same manner as a karate punch. The grip should be held up. This technique can also be executed by striking with the back heads forward for longer extension.

MOROTE-ZUKI
(Double Punch)

Thrust the front heads of both weapons forward (1-3) in the same manner as a karate double punch. The back heads can also be used as the points of contact in this technique.

YAMA-ZUKI
(U-Punch)

Keeping the grip of both tonfa upward, strike the opponent (1-3) in the face and the stomach. The striking point of the tonfa is the front head, but the back head can also be used if one needs a longer reach.

MAE-FURI
(Partial Front Flip Downward)

From a heiko-dachi (1), draw the tonfa up and forward to shoulder level (2) as if executing a punch, while loosening your grip slightly to flip the back head of the tonfa up and over in an arc to strike the target (3&4) with the side edge of the tonfa. Stop the tonfa in mid-swing by tightening your grip, then bring the weapon back (5-7) with a snapping motion of the wrist.

FURI-OTOSHI
(Complete Downward Flip and Back)

Draw the tonfa up (1-3) in the same manner as the mae-furi (partial front flip) but follow through (4&5) with a complete downward swing, striking with the side edge of the tonfa. Strike again (6-8) by bringing the tonfa back up in a circular motion in the reverse direction. In essence, you are first striking overhead and following with an uppercut.

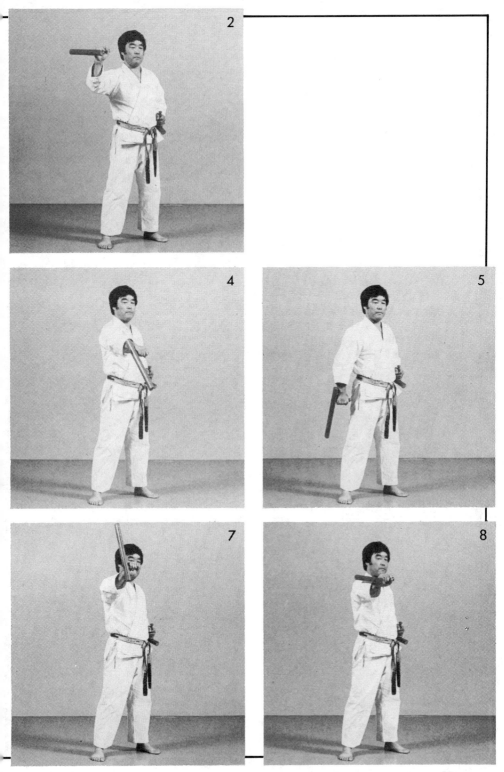

YOKO-FURI
(Complete Sideward Flip)

Using a circular motion, flip the back head of the tonfa (1-4) across the body, striking with the side edge of the weapon. Quickly repeat this motion in reverse (5-7), striking again with the opposite side of the tonfa. This should be one, swift movement, effecting a double blow to the target. At each extreme of the swing, you must tighten your grip on the tonfa to stop the flip and reverse its direction, loosening the grip in your hand to swing it in the other direction.

1

2

3

UCHI-MAE-FURI
(Inside Front Flip)

This strike comes from the inside. For a right hand strike, pivot to the left (1&2), drawing the right arm across the chest and flipping the tonfa out (3&4) with a quick snap of the elbow, connecting with the target and then flipping the tonfa back (5&6). Strike with the side edge.

HACHIJI-MAWASHI-FURI
(Figure-Eight Flip)

This motion combines a downward flip, palm down (1-4), and another downward strike (5-8) with the palm turned over. The two flips together appear as a figure-eight strike when viewed head-on. Remember that your right arm should move swiftly and in one smooth action. Bring the tonfa back (9&10) with the same action.

FURI-BARAI
(Across and Down)

From a heiko-dachi, draw the tonfa around in front of your body (1-3), as you pivot to your left and prepare to strike down and across from your upper left to your lower right (4&5). Flip the tonfa down swiftly and strike the target with the side edge. Retrieve the tonfa (6-8) with a quick flip back to your starting point.

YOKO-KOTE-GAESHI
(Side Flip)

This technique is for changing your grasp on the tonfa from the grip to the body of the tonfa with a side flip. From a heiko-dachi (or natural stance), grasp the tonfa (1) on the grip with your right hand, palm up. Flip the back head counterclockwise (2-4) over the hand and lock your fingers around the main body of the tonfa as it rolls into your palm. The palm should be covering the top side of the tonfa (5), your fingers around the bottom. From here you can now strike with the front head of the tonfa. You can also return the tonfa to the original position easily (6&7) by releasing the tonfa body and catching the grip.

YOKO-KOTE-GAESHI
(Close-Up)

The grasp on the grip of the tonfa (1) is firm, with the palm of the hand up and the back head of the tonfa pointing downward. With a firm, smooth move, flip the bottom head of the tonfa over the hand (2-9) in a counterclockwise direction while releasing your hold on the grip. The hand remains relatively stationary and in the area between the grip and the top side of the tonfa. Roll the palm up and grasp the top side of the tonfa (10). To change the hold on the tonfa back to the original position, bring the main body of the tonfa into a vertical position and release it (11-13). Turn the hand slightly, palm up, as the tonfa drops, grasping the tonfa again by the grip.

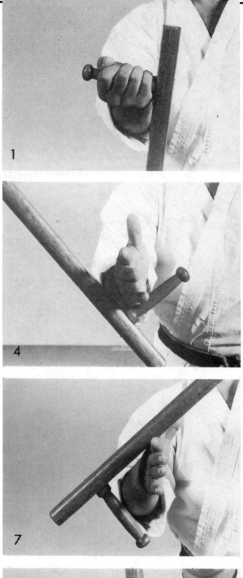

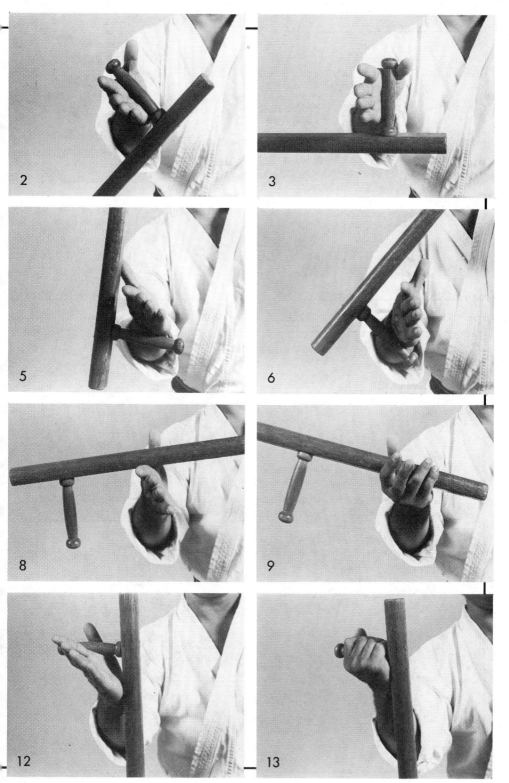

MAE-KOTE-GAESHI
(Front Flip)

This technique is for changing your grasp on the tonfa flipping overhand from front to back (1-3). Hold the tonfa by the grip, back head pointing away from you, in a horizontal position. Flip the back head upward and toward you and grasp the top side of the tonfa with your palm. *Caution:* Do not bend your elbow while executing this move, but use a firm, smooth move.

MAE-KOTE-GAESHI
(Close-Up)

With the tonfa held by the grip, back head pointing away from you (1), flip the tonfa upward and back toward you (2-5). Open your hand quickly so that your fingers point outward and your thumb back toward your body. As the top side of the tonfa touches the hand (thumb side), roll the palm upward and grasp the tonfa's body on the top side. The grip end is now facing (6) your opponent.

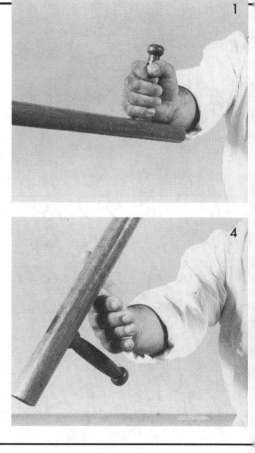

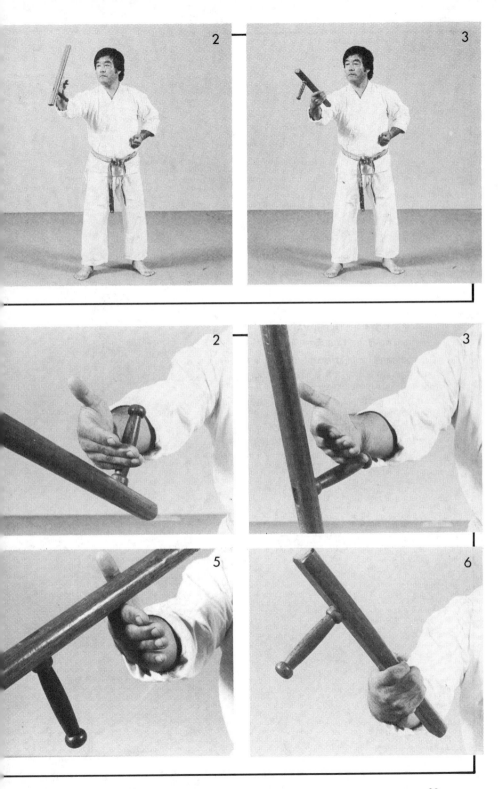

MOROTE-KOTE-MAWASHI
(Two-Hand Circular Flip)

Grasping the tonfa (1) with both hands, one hand on the grip and the other holding the back head of the tonfa, swing the front head around over the top (2-4) quickly, delivering a strike with the side edge. Swing it back in the opposite direction (5-7) to the starting position.

MOROTE-MAI-FURI
(Double Front Flip)

With elbows raised to almost shoulder height (1) and the grips of both tonfa inside your arms, flip the back heads over (2&3) in an arc and stop with the back heads pointed straight

ahead. Retrieve the back heads (4&5) with the same quick motion in reverse. The striking area is the side edge or back head of the tonfa.

1

MOROTE-YOKO-FURI
(Double Side Flip)

(1) From a heiko-dachi position, pivot to your right (2) without shifting your feet and swing both tonfa together (3-7) in one circular sidesweep, striking with the side edge of each weapon.

3

6

MOROTE-HACHIJI-MAWASHI-FURI
(Double Figure-Eight Flip)

This is similar to the single figure-eight flip only performed simultaneously with both hands, beginning with an outside flip (1-5) downward using the elbows quickly to deliver side edge strikes to the opponent. As you flip the tonfa underneath (6&7), turn your wrists out, palms up, to deliver a second downward strike with the tonfa on the inside of your arms. Complete the figure-eight movement (8-11) by turning your grips underneath your palms and flipping the tonfa down again in a strike to your opponent. Retrieve the tonfa (12&13) with a quick flip back into the ready position. This particular technique should be practiced with care, as the tonfa could easily strike the face or be deflected by colliding with the other tonfa.

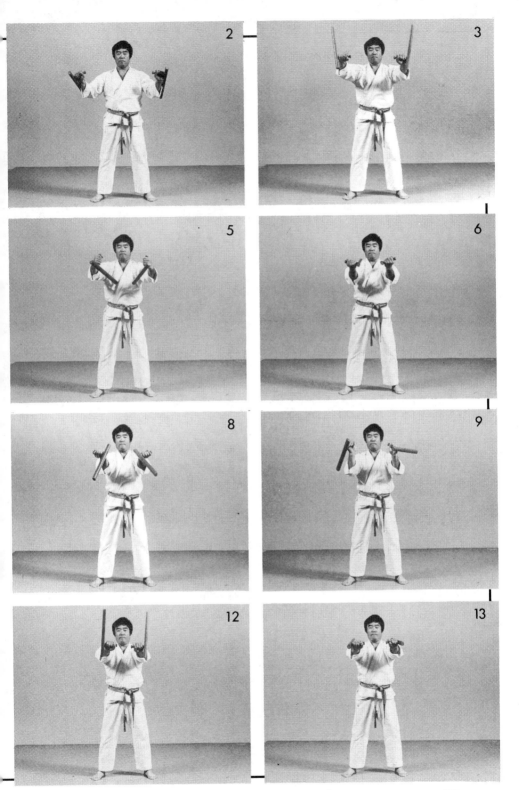

MOROTE-KOSA-FURI
(Double Side Cross Flip)

(1) From a heiko-dachi, extend your arms out simultaneously (2&3), flipping the tonfa in opposite directions from outside to inside, delivering a strike (4&5) with the side edges of the tonfa as they travel around from back to front. Be sure to keep the grips of both tonfa held up. When your arms have crossed, swing your arms back out (6-8) in the reverse of this motion, delivering a second strike identical to the first and returning each tonfa to the starting position. This should be performed as one swift movement.

SELF-DEFENSE APPLICATIONS

The self-defense applications presented here are intended to provide examples of how the tonfa could be utilized under various situations. The proper execution of these techniques depends upon the depth of understanding and degree of skill developed in the previous sections. Effective performance with *ma-ai*, *kime* and *mushin* will help the student develop balance, mobility, speed and power. These are qualities which can be easily transferred to karate and other kobudo weapons.

The key to mastery of the tonfa is constant practice, but always with correct posture, proper stance, and good breathing. The following exercises were chosen especially for the novice as he begins this type of training. The person trained in karate should use his karate basics as a foundation for the tonfa techniques. With a little imagination, the karate student could expand on the following applications by creating combinations developed from the blocks, stances and counters given in the previous sections. One should practice these techniques in all directions—forward, back and both sides. It is important also that the student first master the simpler applications before he tries to proceed to more complex combinations.

AGE-UKE/SEIKEN-ZUKI

(1) As your opponent's right overhead strike with a bo (uchi-otoshi) approaches, slide your left foot back (2) into a right forward stance (zenkutsu-dachi) and block upward with the tonfa (3&4) in the left hand. Use the bottom side of the tonfa for the block. Immediately after contact, forcefully push the bo downward (5&6) with the blocking tonfa and thrust the front head of the right tonfa (7&8) into the opponent's chin.

FURI-UKE/YOKO-FURI

(1) The attack is again a uchi-otoshi (overhead attack with a bo). Side step to your left with the left foot (2) into a forward stance (zenkutsu-dachi) and block upward (3) with the right hand tonfa using an outward flipping block. The side edge of the spinning tonfa (4&5) deflects the bo down and can then be spun immediately in the reverse direction (6-8), flipping the side edge of the tonfa into the opponent's temple.

AGE-UKE/YOKO-FURI

(1) As your opponent's attack with the bo approaches, side step to the left into a left forward stance (2-4) and use an upward block (age-uke) to halt the attack. Reverse your stance and strike the bo downward with the left tonfa (5), drawing the right tonfa back (6), preparing to strike. Flip the right tonfa (7&8) around and strike the opponent's head with the side edge of the tonfa.

KOUSA-UKE/MOROTE-KOSA-FURI

(1) From a right forward stance, step back with the right foot (2) into a left forward stance (3) and block with both tonfa upward in the cross block. Using the right hand tonfa (4&5) to force the bo down and away, draw the left tonfa back preparing to counter. Flip both tonfa (6&7) around to either side of the attacker's head, striking with the side edge of each tonfa closest to the back head end.

MOROTE-UKE/URAKEN/
YOKO-HIJIATE

(1) Your attacker approaches with a two-handed reverse thrust to your mid-section (tsuki-komi). Step back with the left leg (2&3) into the horse stance (kiba-dachi) and use a double forearm block (4) to deflect the bo. Flip the right tonfa (5-7) over the top of your arm into the attacker's face, using a backhand motion. Flip the right tonfa back over (8&9) the side of your arm and then slide into the opponent with your right foot as you strike again (10&11), using a right elbow strike to his midsection. The point of contact should be the back head of the tonfa.

FURI-UKE/YOKO-FURI

(1-4) The attacker tries a reverse strike with the bo to the lower body (gyaku-yoko-uchi). Quickly step to your left into a forward stance (zenkutsu-dachi) and parry with a block using the bottom side of the right tonfa. With a flip of the left tonfa (5-8), strike your opponent's right knee while shifting your stance. Your right tonfa is now back in a prepared position, and you can attack your opponent (9-10) by striking his jaw with a flip of the tonfa, reversing your stance again.

2

3

5

6

9

10

YOKO-KOTE-GAESHI/ WASHITE (OTOSHI)

To strike an opponent with the grip head, you must transfer your grasp on the tonfa from the grip to the back head end. To switch, use a side flip (1-3) to bring

the back head portion of the weapon into your hand, front head pointing up. Strike downward (4&5) using the grip head as the point of contact.

MAE-KOTE-GAESHI/ HIRABASAMI

Change your grasp on the tonfa (1-3) from the grip to the back head by executing a front wrist flip. Now use the vise-like surface to strike your opponent (4-6) in the neck. The grip and front head form an L-shape that can be thrust into your opponent.

MOROTE-KOTE-MAWASHI/ YOKO-FURI

(1) From a left forward stance, block an overhead bo strike using the double-hand flipping technique (morote kote-mawashi, page 70). Force the bo quickly down to the right by

rotating (2&3) your left wrist over your right. Release the tonfa (4) with your left hand and, using a right-handed flip, strike your opponent (5&6) with the side edge of the tonfa.

AGE-UKE/SEIKEN-ZUKI

(1) Assume a defensive posture with the left leg back under the threat of a katana (sword) attack. As soon as the sword is drawn back to strike (2), step forward quickly with your left foot into a forward stance

(zenkutsu-dachi) and block the forearm of the opponent (3) with a left upward block. Using your hips for thrust (4&5), strike with the front head of the right tonfa into the solar plexus of the attacker.

FURI-UKE/FURI-OTOSHI/ YOKO-FURI

This two-tonfa defense is to be used when the katana attack is aimed at your lower body. (1) Assume a right fighting stance, and as your opponent's sweep begins (2), quickly step to the left into a crane stance (sagiashi-dachi) and block the sword (3-5) with a downward flip strike of the right tonfa. Step toward your attacker (6-9) into a forward stance again and strike his sword wrist with a downward flip of the left tonfa. Draw the right tonfa back (10-12) and flip it into the right jaw of your opponent, turning your hips and reversing your stance to follow through with the most power.

FURI-UKE/FURI-OTOSHI/ YOKO-FURI

Assume a right forward stance (1) as your opponent threatens with an over-head katana attack. As the sweep to the upper body begins (2-4), side step to the left into a forward stance (zenkutsu-dachi) and flip block the sword in the opposite direction with the right tonfa, catching the sword on its top side. Reverse your stance quickly (5-7) and strike the sword with a downward flip of the left tonfa, preparing a strike with the right tonfa. Flip the right tonfa (8-10) to the jaw of your attacker with a twist-ing of your hips back into the left for-ward stance to give the blow power.

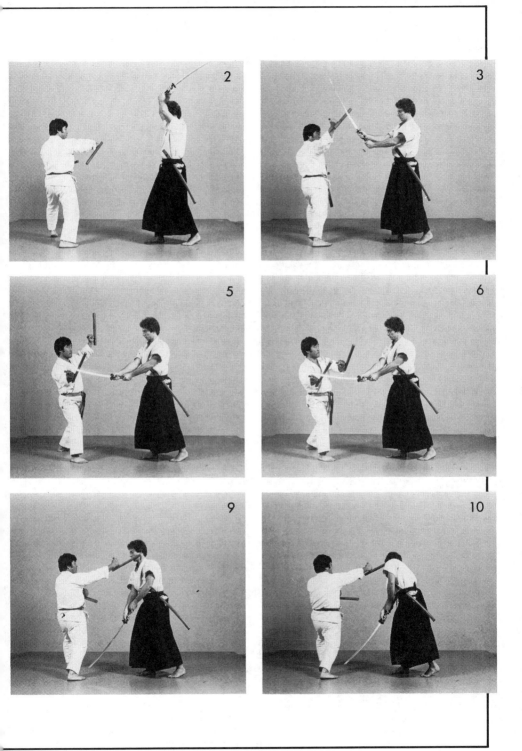

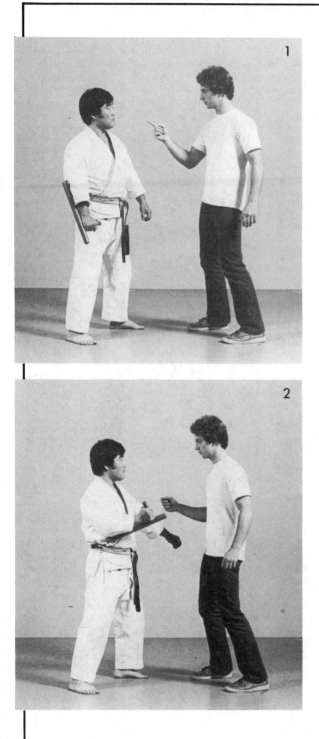

SEIKEN-ZUKI

Using one tonfa, the threat of attack is repelled easily (1-4) by assuming a left forward posture with the tonfa in your right hand and

thrusting the front head of the tonfa directly in the midsection of your opponent. Use your hips to generate greater thrusting power.

FURI-OTOSHI

(1) Assume a defensive posture with the right foot back and the tonfa in the right hand. When an attack becomes imminent, flip the tonfa overhead (2-4) and downward toward the attacker's face. In this instance, the opponent leans back to avoid the strike and begins to attack. Following through with a reverse motion (5-7), flip the tonfa back underneath into his groin area.

YOKO-FURI

(1) When your opponent steps in and threatens you, flip the tonfa around toward the attacker's head (2-5), but actually feigning the strike in preparation for the real one. Drop your body down onto your left knee (6-8) and quickly flip the side edge of the tonfa into your opponent's shin. This will drop him without further strikes.

2

4

5

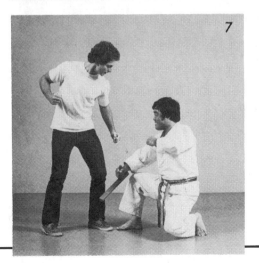

7

8

USHIRO-ZUKI

This is a simple maneuver when you are threatened unexpectedly from the side. With the tonfa in the right hand (1) assume an open-

leg stance (hachiji-dachi). If your opponent reaches for your shoulder (2-5), quickly strike him in the face with the grip head of the tonfa.

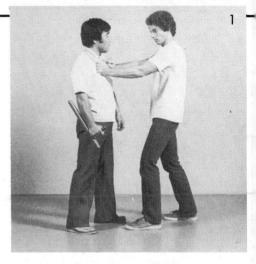

1

MOROTE-OSAE-UKE

Your opponent (1) grabs your shirt or lapel when you are in a left defense posture. Flip the tonfa in your right hand (2-4) over his arms and grab the back head of the tonfa with your left hand (the grip remains in your right hand). Draw the bottom of the tonfa toward you (5&6) applying pressure on the wrists of your attacker. When he is on his knees and has released his hold (7&8), thrust the bottom of the tonfa into his throat.

3

6

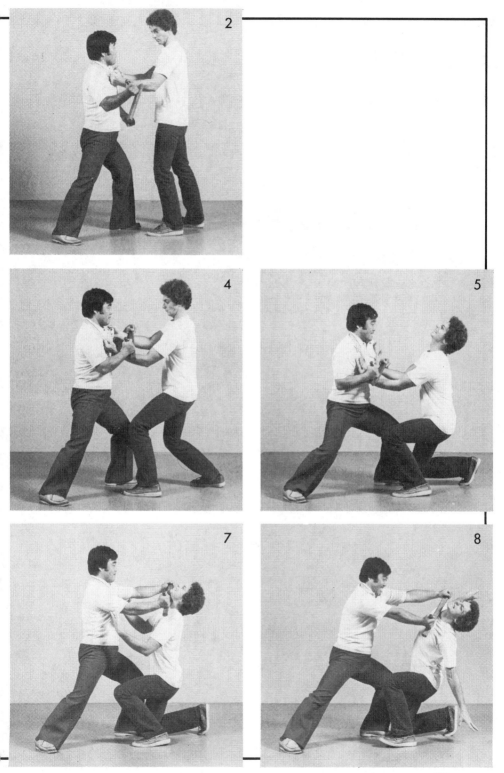

AGE-UKE/KOTE-UCHI

Your opponent grabs your clothing with one hand (1) and prepares to punch with his right hand (2). Use your left arm to execute a karate block (3&4) and force his right arm (5) down and away. Seize his left wrist with your left and strike his elbow with the tonfa in your right hand (6-10). This will force him down to the ground while you maintain a grip on his wrist.

USHIRO-ZUKI/TETTSUI

(1) Your opponent attacks with a rear choke. With the tonfa in your right hand, use the grip head of the tonfa to strike the opponent's face (2-4) directly over your shoulder. Drop your body

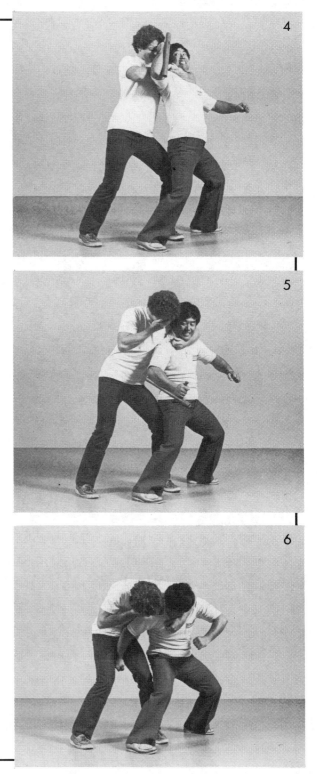

down to widen your stance and gain balance. Bring the tonfa down rapidly (5&6) to strike the opponent in the groin using the bottom of the tonfa.

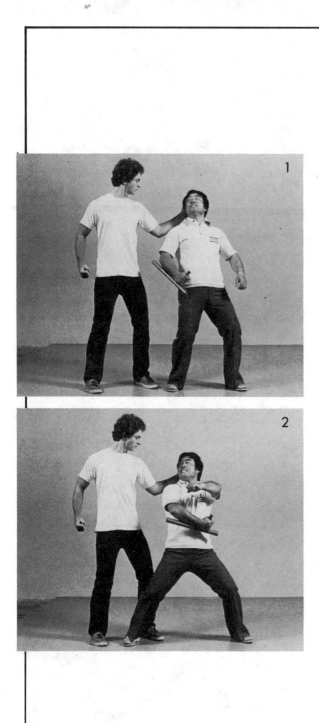

USHIRO-ZUKI/AGE-ZUKI/HIJIATE

(1) The opponent attacks by grabbing the hair from behind. Strike the attacker's chest with the grip head of the tonfa (2-4), dropping

your body weight and widening your stance slightly. Using the front head, strike the attacker's chin (5-7) in an upper cut

Continued on next page

Continued from previous page

motion. Move your right arm outward (8-10) and thrust the back head of the tonfa into the opponent's chest, using your left hand

to add thrusting power to the blow. This maneuver demonstrates how all ends of the tonfa may be used to good effect.

TEISHO-UKE/HEIKO-ZUKI/KAKETE

When an attack is imminent, assume a defense posture (1) with the tonfa in your left hand. As the opponent reaches out (2) to grab and kick you, block downward (3&4) into the knee or shin with both hands supporting the tonfa—your right hand grasping the side near the back head, your left hand on the grip. Draw the tonfa back toward your chest (5-7) and into the attacker's chin in a swift, upward motion. Take your left hand off the grip of the tonfa (8-10) and move it near the bottom (the back head) next to your right hand. Hook the opponent's neck from behind with the grip and pull with both hands down, delivering a smash with a knee lift to the face.

1

SEIKEN-ZUKI/KAKETE/ WASHITE (OTOSHI)

(1) Seized from behind in a two-hand hair grab, step back with the left foot (2) in the direction of the pull, pivoting across the attacker's body and dropping your body down to your right knee (3) as you turn. With the tonfa in your right hand, strike (4-6) with the front head into the groin. Grasp the tonfa on the longer end near the back head with both hands and hook the attacker's left knee (7&8) with the tonfa grip. Pull his left leg forward and up as you stand up, knocking him on his back (9&10). Use the grip head (11&12) to strike him in the groin using both hands and dropping your weight into the blow.

4

7

10

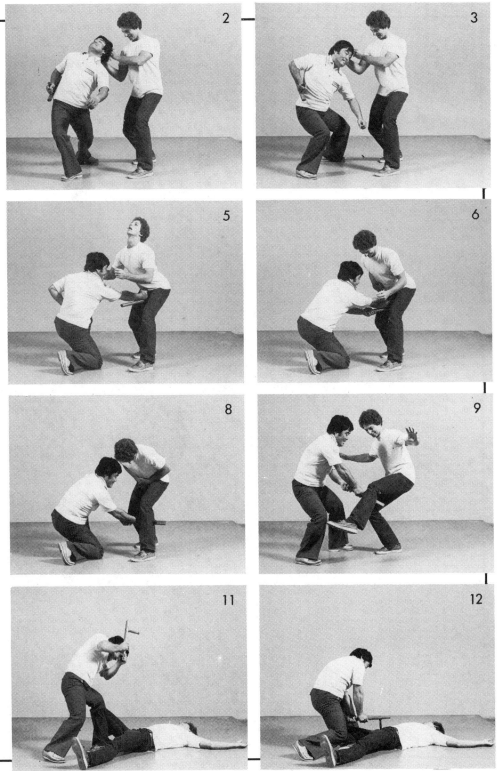

MOROTE-KOTE-MAWASHI/ YOKO-FURI

Assume a defensive posture if you are being threatened (1) holding the tonfa with the right hand on the grip, the left hand on the side near the back head. When your opponent tries to shove you with his left hand (2), deflect it with a forearm block, using the bottom of the tonfa (3-5) to force his arm down and away. Release your left hand grasp on the side of the tonfa and flip (6-8) with the right hand, striking the opponent's jaw or temple.

KOTE-JIME

This is a simple maneuver to use if someone grabs your wrist which is holding the tonfa (1-3). If he grabs your right wrist with his left hand, lock his hand onto your wrist with your left hand (4-5) while raising your right wrist in a counterclockwise fashion. Circle the tonfa (6-8) over your opponent's wrist and apply pressure to the wrist.

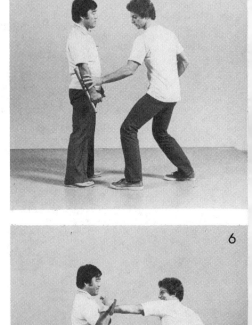

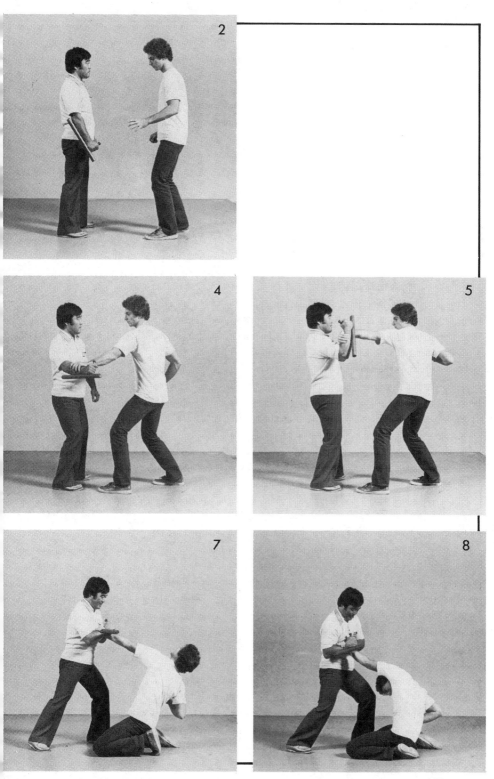

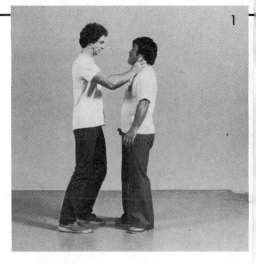

AGE-ZUKI/TETTSUI

The opponent grabs your throat (1) with both hands while the tonfa is in your right hand. Step back (2-5) with your left leg into a side stance (kiba-dachi) and thrust the front head of the tonfa into the attacker's chin. Pull the opponent's right hand away from your neck as you execute this strike, then circle the tonfa downward (6-9) and strike with the bottom edge of the tonfa into his groin.

 2

 3

 5

 6

 8

 9

TEISHO-UKE/NUKITE

(1) From a right defense, step backward with your right foot (2) into a left forward stance (zenkutsu-dachi) and use a downward block (3) to stop the attack. Keep the right hand on the tonfa grip and the left across the top near the back head. Draw the tonfa back and thrust (4-8) the back head into the attacker's face to counter.

HACHIJI-MAWASHI-FURI

As your attacker approaches with a knife ready to thrust at your midsection (1), assume a left forward stance with the tonfa in the right hand. When the attacker begins to thrust (2-4) side step to your left into a left forward stance and block the attack with an outward flip block downward. Circle the tonfa back and around (5-8) into the attacker's head, striking with the back head side of the tonfa.

NAGASHI/HIRABASAMI/KAKETE

When the attacker threatens with a knife (1), assume a left forward stance while holding the tonfa near the bottom (back head). As the attacker lunges forward (2-4), parry his thrust with a downward strike to his knife wrist, using the area between the grip and the top (front head) of the tonfa as the striking point. Draw the tonfa back and thrust it into the neck of your opponent (5) using the same striking area of the tonfa. Use the grip head to grab the opponent (6) behind the back of the neck and pull him forward and down (7&8) into a right front snap kick to the groin.

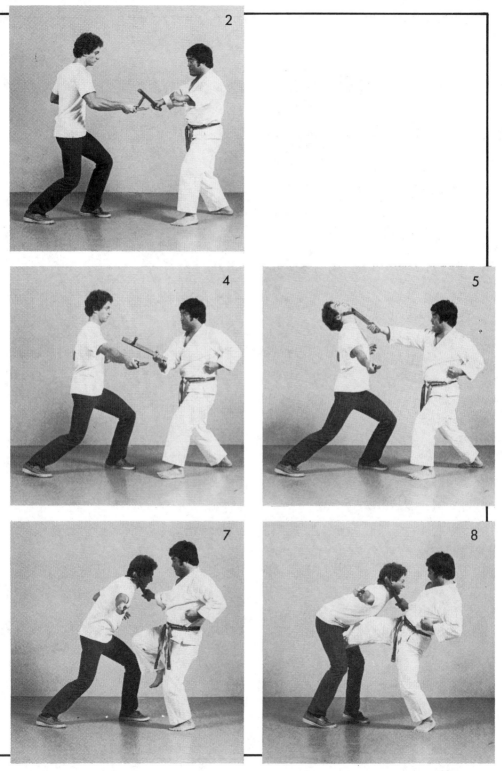

SOTO-MAWASHI-UKE

When your opponent threatens with a slashing knife attack (1), assume a left forward stance, holding the tonfa near the bottom (back head). Counter his slashing motion (2-4) by striking his hand with the grip of the tonfa, hooking the grip over the top of his wrist and (5-7) swinging the tonfa in an arc counterclockwise. Draw the tonfa back (8-11) and use the grip head once more to strike the midsection of your attacker.

UCHI-MAWASHI-UKE

(1) When your opponent prepares to thrust with a downward knife strike, assume a left forward stance with the tonfa held in your right hand near the back head. When he steps forward with his attack (2-4) pivot to the left and strike his attacking hand with the top edge of the tonfa. Hook his wrist (5-7) using the grip of the tonfa and circle his knife arm down counterclockwise and back up into his midsection.